IMAGES
of America

CAMP DODGE

A 7th Service Command Military Police motorcycle escort leads a vehicle column of U.S. Army quarter-ton jeeps and two-and-a-half-ton trucks through the main gate of Camp Dodge around 1943. (Courtesy of the Iowa Gold Star Military Museum, Camp Dodge, Iowa.)

On the cover: Walking behind the iconic company mess halls of Camp Dodge, officers and men of the World War II Armed Forces Induction Station wear a variety of field clothing and gear of the type issued to the over 70,000 U.S. Army recruits inducted at Camp Dodge. (Courtesy of the Iowa Gold Star Military Museum, Camp Dodge, Iowa.)

IMAGES
of America

CAMP DODGE

Mary L. Jones and Michael W. Vogt

ARCADIA
PUBLISHING

ISBN 978-0-7385-6091-5

Published by Arcadia Publishing
Charleston, South Carolina

Printed in the United States of America

Library of Congress Control Number: 2008943472

For all general information contact Arcadia Publishing at:
Telephone 843-853-2070
Fax 843-853-0044
E-mail sales@arcadiapublishing.com
For customer service and orders:
Toll-Free 1-888-313-2665

Visit us on the Internet at www.arcadiapublishing.com

Dedicated to the memory of the first three
Iowa Gold Star Military Museum directors:
Aloysius Rolfes
Thomas Bolton
Jerry Gorden
Their vision was our inspiration

Contents

ACKNOWLEDGMENTS

The authors would like to acknowledge the assistance given to them during the writing of this book.

Special thanks go to Col. (retired) Russell Bierl, Iowa Gold Star Military Museum director, for his research and assistance with this project and Col. (retired) Bob Thomas for sharing his wealth of historical knowledge and for relating details on Camp Dodge that only his unique personal experience could provide.

Providing research assistance were Chief Warrant Officer 3 (retired) Wesley Bender, Arlen Ciechanowski, Dana Grefe, Ron Gruber, Lt. Col. Greg Hapgood, Stephen Ransom, and Hank Zalatel. Thanks also go to Camp Dodge employee Fred Sheeks, who is always willing to share the knowledge gained from his half-century of employment on the post.

Assisting with editing were Lt. Col. (retired) Gaylen Heaberlin, Curtis Madsen, M.Sgt. Duff McFadden, and Lt. Col. (retired) Michael Musel.

The following sources were of particular assistance in researching Camp Dodge history: Camp Dodge reference and photograph files, Iowa Gold Star Military Museum Library, Camp Dodge. The *Camp Dodger* newspaper, published from September 21, 1917, to January 31, 1919. The *Iowa Guardsman* and *Iowa Militiaman* magazines, published from 1923 to the present. The *Report of the Adjutant General*, published by the State of Iowa, Des Moines, for the years 1900–2008.

And lastly, thanks go to the many photographers, past and present, who determined that the personnel and activities at Camp Dodge were worthy of placing before their lenses.

Unless otherwise noted, all images appear courtesy of the Iowa Gold Star Military Museum. The authors' portion of royalties from this book will benefit the Iowa National Guard Memorial Association.

INTRODUCTION

The photographs in this book represent a minor sampling of rarely seen Camp Dodge images from the Iowa Gold Star Military Museum's archive and depict a story 100 years in the making.

The post is primarily known as the home of the Iowa National Guard. However, few know the full history of this remarkable place and the many individuals and organizations that have played a role in its colorful past. A future president swam in the post's Olympic-sized outdoor pool. A future five-star general missed his first chance at deploying for combat from here. Iowa's first World War I combat casualty passed his U.S. Army physical here. Former presidents came to rally World War I soldiers. Some 90 years later, a vice president rallied another generation of men and women in their fight against terrorism.

The post has seen many architectural, spatial, and organizational changes over the years. It began as a small area where Iowa National Guard troops conducted military maneuvers and small arms practice. Camp Dodge was converted by the Department of War for use as a regular U.S. Army training cantonment during World War I and an induction station during World War II. The post has been temporary home to a school, a university annex, and a nursing home. A small town, once a stop on the electric Inter-Urban Railway to Perry, is now a mock city in the center of the military reservation used for the training of law enforcement, emergency personnel, and soldiers conducting military operations in urban terrain. Buildings housing high-tech communications, the state's Homeland Security and Emergency Management Division, and computer battle simulators sit on land once used for training cavalry horses. Military veterans find assistance at the Department of Veterans Affairs and the Iowa National Guard Records Center. Currently the Iowa National Guard—both Army and Air—maintain their headquarters on the post.

Leadership and training activities have played a key role at Camp Dodge throughout the years. Young men have learned from the leadership activities provided by the American Legion's Hawkeye Boys State since 1938. The Iowa Military Academy (IMA) began at Camp Dodge in 1957 and celebrated its 50th anniversary in 2007 as the renamed 185th Regiment, Regional Training Institute (RTI). The Iowa Law Enforcement Academy (ILEA), opened in 1970, provides year-round instruction to the state's peace officers. Law enforcement agencies ranging from local police to the FBI use the post's target ranges and other facilities. The camp is home to the Midwest Counter Drug Training Center, which offers courses to assist those involved in fighting drug trafficking and substance abuse. Soldiers from across the country come to Camp Dodge to receive instruction at the U.S. Army's National Maintenance Training Center.

The short history that follows illustrates what actually happened at Camp Dodge. But the post's history is also replete with forgotten stories regarding what did not occur. After World War I, Camp Dodge was seen as an area teeming with possibilities. The Des Moines Chamber of Commerce proposed that the post be developed as an industrial center with factories established on-site. A 1922 news article referenced a movement to build a memorial hospital in honor of doctors, nurses, and others who died at Camp Dodge during the war with funding by subscription. In 1942, the Iowa American Legion recommended that Camp Dodge host a 100-bed hospital for war veterans with tuberculosis. Although these plans and others never reached fruition, they demonstrate that the surrounding communities viewed the post as a valuable asset worth developing.

It is also difficult to separate Camp Dodge from the communities that surround it. The City of Des Moines was of prime importance, particularly during the post's early years. When Iowa's capital city moved west to Des Moines from Iowa City in 1857, the office of the adjutant general moved with it. Appointed by the governor to serve as the head of the Iowa militia, and later the Iowa National Guard, the adjutant general oversaw the funding and training of the organization. A central location accessible by rail was a priority when finally deciding on a main training area for the state. Des Moines then promoted Camp Dodge as a site for one of the World War I cantonments (a cantonment being an area providing military quarters). The city was a source of labor and materials for its construction. The community supported the soldiers, providing lodging for visitors, entertainment, and needed supplies. The fact that Fifty-eighth Street was the main road from Des Moines to camp led the city council to name it for Merle D. Hay, Iowa's first World War I combat death. The small town of Herrold, founded in 1906, became a boomtown during World War I, offering a rail stop, shops, and entertainment just north of the post. It was also Camp Dodge's first mailing address. Its nearby location finally became its downfall when the post's ranges were moved and the range safety fan came dangerously close. It was then purchased by the federal government and became part of Camp Dodge.

Several towns, Dodge City and Army City, were born to serve the World War I camp, and they disappeared almost as quickly as the World War I cantonment did. Nearby Johnston grew and thrived in the shadow of Camp Dodge. Johnston Station, many times misspelled on historic maps as "Johnson," started as a rail stop south of the post in 1906. It became a thriving community serving both Camp Dodge and the Pioneer Hi-Bred Corn Company, which became the leading seed corn producer in the world. Although it was not formally incorporated as a city until 1969, it is now one of the fastest growing cities in Iowa.

Due to space limitations, many important facts, photographs, and people were regrettably omitted from this volume. We invite you to visit the Iowa Gold Star Military Museum to learn more about the post's history and share your own stories of Camp Dodge's past.

As Camp Dodge begins its second century, it is difficult to imagine the changes the future will bring, but that is, of course, a story for future historians to interpret.

One

The Beginnings 1905–1916

On April 12, 1909, the State of Iowa's first purchase took place for land that would become Camp Dodge, the permanent home of the Iowa National Guard. This had been no easy process. Before this, annual training camps were held throughout the state, creating some problems with host communities. In 1901, costly private property destruction caused by drunken and unruly soldiers convinced Adj. Gen. Melvin Byers that a permanent campground was needed. He called for a centralized camp near the state capital, Des Moines. Also located near Des Moines was a U.S. Army installation, Fort Des Moines.

In 1904, the state purchased 160 acres next to Fort Des Moines. The ground was seeded and temporary buildings erected. The site was used for two years, but officials decided that the ground was not dry enough or level enough for use by all of the regiments at once.

When the federal government purchased 320 acres for a shooting range northwest of Des Moines in 1906, the Iowa National Guard decided to sell the state-owned acres next to Fort Des Moines and purchase land next to the new range.

By 1908, the improvements to the federal range were completed, but the Iowa National Guard still had not sold its land south of town. One alternative, purchasing part of the existing federal range, was dismissed because of the distance—two miles—from the Inter-Urban Railway. This distance made moving troops and equipment (and visitors) cumbersome and time-consuming.

Finally land close to the Inter-Urban Railway was located, and purchases started in 1909. In 1910, Adj. Gen. Guy Logan directed the post be named Camp Dodge to honor Maj. Gen. Grenville M. Dodge, one of Iowa's Civil War heroes.

Although one regiment held its annual encampment there in 1911, the first statewide encampment was held in 1914. The post continued to grow, and by 1916, the state owned about 230 acres of land.

Meanwhile a war was raging in Europe, with the United States reluctant to enter. However, when a threat came from Mexico, National Guard troops were called into federal service. Iowa National Guardsmen mustered at Camp Dodge before deployment to Texas. Although Iowa troops did not see combat, field training there prepared them for a larger confrontation about to move the United States onto the world stage.

Tents are readied for the 2nd Brigade in this 1882 photograph of Camp Bentley near the Waterloo fairgrounds. Before Camp Dodge was established, annual camps were held at various locations throughout the state, sometimes for a single regiment, sometimes for the entire Iowa National Guard. Calls for a permanent campground that would save labor on setup and striking camp, leaving more time for military training, came as early as 1890.

This is a company of the 56th Infantry Regiment, Iowa National Guard, at Camp Cummings located on grounds near Fort Des Moines during its annual training period, July 6–13, 1905. The state purchased 160 acres north of Fort Des Moines in 1904 and conducted training activities there in 1904 and 1905. Annual encampment names were usually chosen to honor a noteworthy soldier or leader.

A postcard view of the 1906 campground for the 53rd Regiment shows an area near Maquoketa in eastern Iowa. Soldiers enjoyed the variety found in varying annual training sites. Both guardsmen and their host communities viewed the camps as eagerly anticipated training and social events, with parades through the town, military balls, and townsfolk trekking to the campsites to view military drills and sporting events.

Adj. Gen. Melvin Byers, a Civil War veteran, led the Iowa National Guard through the Spanish-American War and into the new century. Byers realized the need for a permanent camp, favoring a central location. Rival cities were incensed, particularly representatives from Cedar Rapids, who already had an Iowa National Guard rifle range. Dissension grew, and the issue became Byers's downfall in 1905. His successor, William H. Thrift, also lost his position due to support for a central camp.

Iowa National Guard troops bivouac at Camp Bowen, near the future site of Camp Dodge, during the August 5–12, 1907, "Iowa Maneuvers." The exercises involved the entire Iowa National Guard, training jointly with units of the U.S. Army. The Iowa National Guard and U.S. Army units were divided into "Blue" and "Brown" armies, pitted against each other in a series of tactical exercises and mock skirmishes on land northeast of present-day Camp Dodge.

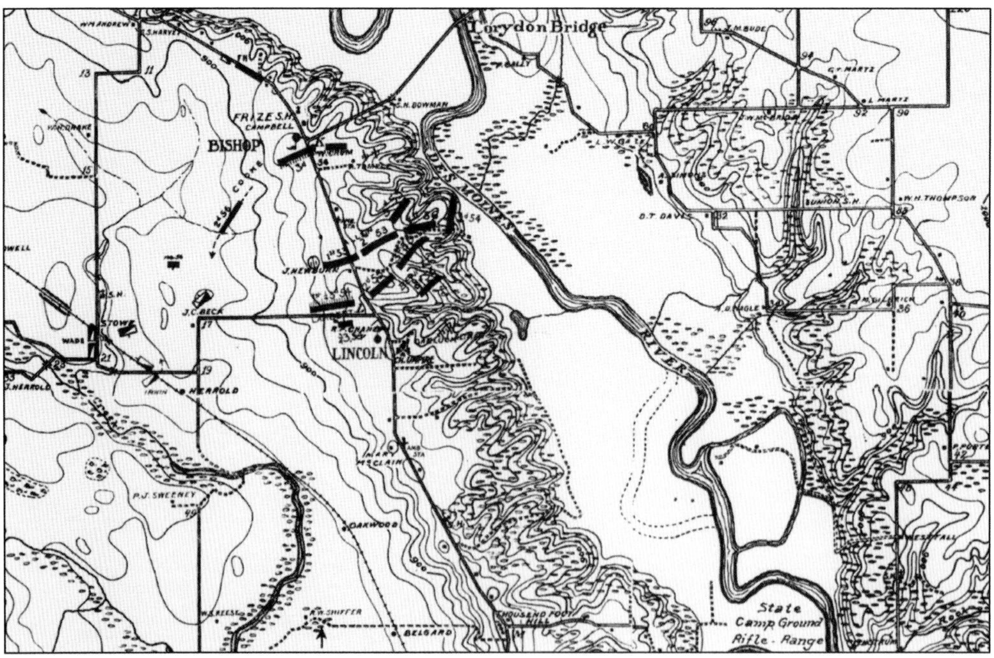

A map created in 1907 during the documentation of the Blue versus Brown training maneuvers shows the federally owned state campground and rifle range on the lower right. Future Camp Dodge would be located directly west, near the hatched rail line. The town of Herrold, north on the Inter-Urban Railway, would be listed as the post's first mailing address, changing later to Grimes and finally Johnston.

Overlaid on a satellite image of modern Camp Dodge, the first 1909 land purchase is outlined in white, with its eastern border along Northwest Beaver Drive and its western border along the Inter-Urban Railway. The dark squares show the layout of World War I buildings, now gone. Historic maps label Beaver Drive with many names, including River, Ridge, Beaver, or Camp Dodge Road, as well as Iowa Highway 89, 141, or 401.

The land purchased for Camp Dodge was located north of the Hyperion Field and Motor Club, a social group organized in 1900. The club established a golf course by 1907 and built its clubhouse (left) in 1909 just off Beaver Road (now Drive). As troops prepared to leave for Texas in 1916, visitors in over 3,000 cars created an eight-mile-long traffic jam along this road. To the right are storefronts, likely part of Army City. (Courtesy of the Iowa Department of Transportation.)

Armed with .30-caliber bolt-action M1903 Springfield rifles, soldiers of Company K, 56th Regiment, Emmetsburg, pose for a photograph in July 1911. The 56th Regiment was the first to use Camp Dodge for their annual encampment. Following the 1902 federal reforms of the National Guard, the Iowa National Guard received uniforms and equipment of the same type as used by the regular U.S. Army.

Each year, soldiers of the Iowa National Guard occupied canvas tents for 10-day periods during annual training. An August 1914 photograph exhibits the typical arrangement of the training billets and, at left, shows troops practicing close order drill on the parade ground. The brick farmhouse, part of the original series of land acquisitions, is visible in the background. Records indicate that 1914 was the first all–Iowa National Guard encampment at Camp Dodge.

In August 1915, 3rd Regiment troops stand in company formation during annual training. The wooden mess halls uphill from the company tents would be replaced in the mid-1920s with permanent brick structures.

While the United States avoided entering the on-going war in Europe, another threat was coming from the southern border. When Pancho Villa attacked a U.S. Army garrison in New Mexico, the United States retaliated, calling National Guard troops into federal service. Caissons, limbers, and cannons of Davenport's Battery B, 1st Iowa Field Artillery Regiment, mustered with other Iowa units at Camp Dodge prior to their deployment to Brownsville, Texas, in 1916.

While waiting for deployment to Texas, the soldiers spent part of their July 4 waiting a mounted officer's review, standing in formation on the parade grounds. On July 13, a lightning storm injured 10 soldiers, destroyed 50 tents and left roads knee-deep in water.

The Inter-Urban Railway running through Camp Dodge allowed family, friends, and curious citizens to visit the soldiers and observe the military training activities conducted at camp. This July 23, 1916, photograph was taken during the time period (July 19–25) that the troops were leaving for Texas.

This pre–World War I photograph shows a view of Camp Dodge from the Inter-Urban Railway looking north. The building next to the tracks was the first permanent military building constructed on the post, the North Arsenal. The barn and house on the right were also owned by the National Guard. The adjutant general's 1916 annual report listed ownership of 230 acres containing six frame farmhouses and one brick house, plus noted the construction of the arsenal and 12 mess halls.

Adj. Gen. Guy Logan was a Spanish-American War veteran from southwest Iowa. Like his predecessors, Logan supported a Des Moines area campground and helped it become a reality. Land fitting the Iowa National Guard's needs was located, with purchases starting in 1909. In 1910, Logan issued General Order No. 9, naming the post for Maj. Gen. Grenville M. Dodge. (Courtesy of the State Historical Society of Iowa, Des Moines.)

Major General Dodge was one of Iowa's foremost industrialists and Civil War heroes. After settling in Council Bluffs in 1855, he equipped and organized the Council Bluffs Guards, later known as the Dodge Light Guard. He organized the 4th Iowa Infantry early in the Civil War and later commanded the XVI Corps during Gen. William Tecumseh Sherman's Atlanta campaign. After the war, he was chief engineer of the Union Pacific's portion of the transcontinental railroad. Dodge died in 1916 at the age of 84.

Two

THE WORLD WAR I YEARS 1917–1920

In 1917, the U.S. Army was looking for a few good cities.

The task of training soldiers to join the fight in Europe was monumental and the U.S. Army required 16 new training camps across the country. Cities jumped into the competition to host the camps, among them Des Moines. On June 15, 1917, Des Moines was selected as the site of the 13th National Cantonment. Once it was chosen, construction began almost immediately. The post went from a quiet National Guard training area to a bustling army city.

From September 1917 through December 1918, more than 118,000 soldiers, including 37,111 Iowans, were inducted at Camp Dodge. The camp contained just over 1,500 buildings, more than 10,000 horses and mules, a power plant, a 500-bed hospital, and training ranges. A separate part of the post was set aside for African American soldiers, some from Iowa and surrounding states, but a majority sent from southern states.

An incident involving five African American soldiers, a young telephone operator, and her fiancé, both white, marred the history of the cantonment. On May 24, 1918, the soldiers were accused of approaching the couple as they sat on a hillside. According to testimony, the woman was raped by several soldiers while the fiancé was restrained and beaten. Military justice was swift and final. Four of the soldiers were arrested; the fifth was never charged. All four were tried within five days, and three were condemned to death. All soldiers were to be present for the hanging, with the African Americans ordered to the front. It was a scene long remembered by all the soldiers and an incident that still haunts the history of Camp Dodge.

In October 1918, the Spanish Influenza epidemic swept through camp. Thousands of soldiers were taken ill and 702 died. Then, as swiftly as it began, the epidemic ran its course.

Some 18 months after the United States entered the war, hostilities ended. In December 1918, the camp became a demobilization facility. Over 208,000 midwestern soldiers were discharged from Camp Dodge.

An overview of the post, looking to the northwest, shows the expanse of the camp during World War I. Camp Dodge was home to the 88th Infantry Division, formed in August 1917, and the 19th Infantry Division, formed in the fall of 1918. The 88th Infantry Division served as a replacement division, training 48,490 men for service with other divisions until July 1918. It was then recruited to full strength, deploying to France and service on the western front.

The "city center" of World War I Camp Dodge is shown in this air view taken in 1919. Soldiers would congregate here to enjoy leisure time, viewing movies and shows at the Liberty Theatre, meeting visitors at the Hostess House, reading at the service clubs' libraries, or perhaps composing a letter home in the writing rooms. The view looks to the southeast.

Camp Dodge was chosen as the site of the 13th National Cantonment in June 1917. Construction began almost immediately. The U.S. Army was ready with standardized plans, but local labor provided the force that built the giant post. A local company, Charles Weitz' Sons, was awarded general contractor status. The company met every deadline imposed by the Department of War and completed the project under budget.

Members of Iowa City's Company A, 1st Iowa Engineer Battalion, Iowa National Guard, pose west of the brick farmhouse at Camp Dodge on August 23, 1917. The unit was mustered into federal service on June 30, 1917, and directed to assist with the planning and mapping of the 88th Infantry Division cantonment before deploying to Camp Cody, New Mexico. The 1st Iowa Engineers would later be renamed the 109th Engineer Battalion of the 34th Infantry Division.

This massive one-million-gallon storage reservoir was part of the water system built for the World War I cantonment. Located at the top of the hill on Beaver Road between the firing ranges and Camp Dodge proper, the "temporary" wood and concrete structure served Camp Dodge for over 90 years. The reservoir and the brick house (below) serve as location landmarks in many vintage photographs. For many years, the road from Des Moines was paved only to this corner.

This brick farmhouse was part of the pre–World War I land purchases. Built in 1873 of locally fired brick, it was originally the home of John and Florida White and their seven children. It was purchased by the state in 1910. Since then, it has been modified and enlarged for use by the military. In World War I, it first served as temporary post headquarters.

A World War I–era photograph looks northwest across the southern tip of the troop barracks at Camp Dodge. A segregated U.S. Army required the African American troops and instructors of the 366th Infantry Regiment to be placed in a separate section of the cantonment, located at the southern end of the post.

Returning from field training, soldiers cross the Inter-Urban Railway tracks near the Camp Dodge medical supply depot. Of the 16 U.S. Army cantonment camps built for training inductees, only Camp Dodge was constructed along the route of an electric rail line. The use of an existing line expedited the delivery of supplies to the three depots in camp. Because the Inter-Urban Railway was electric, steam locomotives were used for switching freight cars to the sidings, which were not electrified.

Chicago photographers Arthur Mole and John Thomas came to the post in August 1918. The two were known for their dramatic patriotic photographs taken on military posts throughout the country. Set-up for this event took days, with the image, in proper perspective, being outlined on the ground with marking tape and then lined with blocks on the day of shooting, August 22. All this was directed from the top of a 40-foot tower. The line-up for the photograph started at 1:00 p.m. With temperatures ranging in the 90s and the soldiers dressed in woolen uniforms, 12 soldiers fainted and had to be taken from the field before the photograph was taken at 2:30 p.m. Taken just southwest of the brick arsenals, this photograph of 18,000 men forming the Statue of Liberty became the most famous photographic image taken at Camp Dodge.

Soldiers pose on the second floor of a 200-man company barracks. Over 150 company barracks were constructed at Camp Dodge by the end of World War I. Each barracks contained a dormitory on the second floor furnished with cots or steel bed frames. The first floor included a kitchen, mess hall, and noncommissioned officers' quarters.

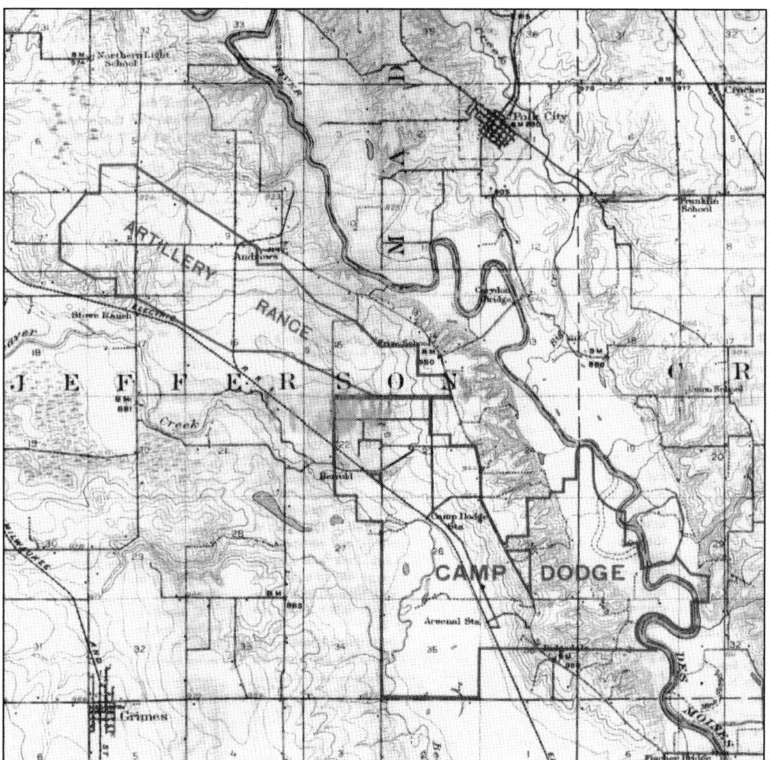

This 1918 map shows the post during World War I. Firing ranges were still located on the east edge of camp by the Des Moines River; farmland to the north was rented as part of the artillery range. The "heart" of the post was located at Camp Dodge Station, now part of the firing range safety fan. The Statue of Liberty photograph was taken to the left of Arsenal Station, in the lower center of the map.

Seeking to avoid the temptations of liquor, prostitution, and gambling, which had plagued camps in prior wars, the U.S. Army worked closely with groups such as the YMCA, Knights of Columbus, Lutheran Brotherhood, and the Jewish Welfare Society to provide soldiers with wholesome activities. The post was filled with service clubs, a theater, and outdoor areas for sports activities. Shown above is the "Red Triangle," or YMCA, Auditorium, site of lectures and concerts.

The YWCA Hostess House was one of the places on the post where female family members could visit with soldiers. A "receiving hostess" and staff of volunteers oversaw the facility, which provided many homelike amenities. It was also the site of weddings, as well as a haven for emergency stays. Former president Theodore Roosevelt visited in 1918 and pronounced it "one of the finest in the nation."

The 5,000-seat Liberty Theatre offered movies and plays and even had its own "soldier orchestra." The most popular offerings were the plays, many of which starred the soldiers themselves. This Liberty Theatre was located on Camp Dodge, but there was another Liberty theater located in Dodge City, a small town that had sprung up on the post's eastern border. To avoid confusion, the theater in Dodge City was renamed the Trilby.

The 60-by-90-foot Lutheran Brotherhood building had a large social room and auditorium. It also served as a site for religious services. It was designed by Des Moines architect Frank E. Wetherell, who also designed the 1915 Camp Dodge North Arsenal Building.

During World War I, horses and mules fulfilled a majority of the U.S. Army's transportation needs. Above, soldiers drive a four-mule hitch at the Remount Station on the west side of Camp Dodge, where over 10,000 horses and mules were trained for service during the war.

Gasoline-powered trucks entered service with the U.S. Army prior to World War I. Posing in the December snow, men of Truck Company 346 acclimate their vehicles and themselves to Iowa's winter temperatures.

Army basic training at Camp Dodge stressed small arms marksmanship, physical fitness, hand-to-hand combat, and bayonet use. French instructors visited Camp Dodge and advised their American allies on the tactics of trench warfare. In the above photograph, Camp Dodge trainees prepare for future combat in the trenches of France.

Recruits are read the camp rules as part of this outdoor classroom session. Many of the new soldiers could not read or write. In addition, a number of them were immigrants who could not speak English. Because of this, classes included not only military training, but also basic reading, writing, and English lessons for those who needed it.

On June 15, 1917, the first training camp for African American officers was established at nearby Fort Des Moines, with former Camp Dodge commander Col. Charles C. Ballou in command. Following the success of the Fort Des Moines Black Officer Candidate School, the 92nd Infantry Division Officers Training School began instruction at Camp Dodge in May 1918, with many of the Fort Des Moines graduates serving as instructors. (Courtesy of the State Historical Society of Iowa, Des Moines.)

A segregated cantonment for African American soldiers was formed at the south end of the post. Although some were from Iowa and surrounding states, the majority were from the South. When 6,000 Alabama soldiers arrived in October 1917, the community expressed many misgivings. However, once the troops arrived, all commented on their "splendid appearance." The local African American community formed organizations to help the soldiers adapt to military life in the North.

The hospital was the only part of the post that was not segregated. Because many soldiers came from the southern states, there was concern that they would not be able to stand the cold Iowa winters and would become ill. However, the decision was made by the U.S. Army to send them north because it was feared that southern opposition to African American soldiers fighting in the war would create conflict. Their treatment at Camp Dodge, while not equal to white soldiers, was at least better than many other camps. In Camp Alexandria, Virginia, 20 African American soldiers froze to death in their canvas tent. The patients below spent some of their time outside, smoking while sitting on what are likely building materials for the post. Construction took place at a frantic pace but could not keep up with the occupancy by military personnel.

The 500-bed hospital complex, located just north of the small town of Herrold, was an important part of the self-contained city that was Camp Dodge. Medical and military personnel recognized the importance of fresh air provided by widely spaced wards and porches. In addition, multiple wards allowed the separation of patients with different illnesses, so that diseases could not spread as easily.

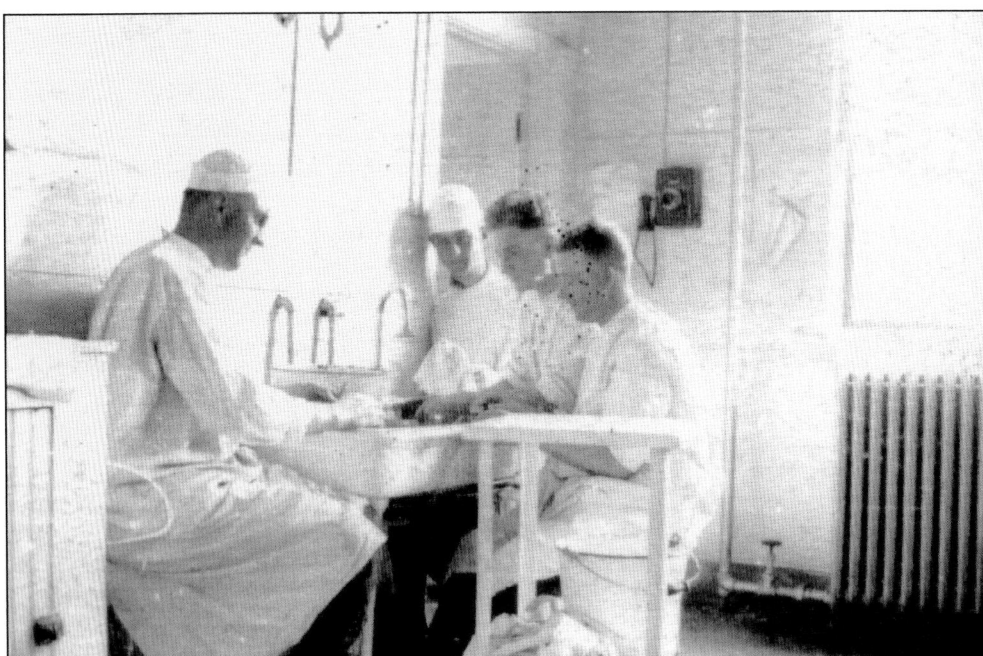

Army hospitals provided the best in sanitation that the times could provide. Steam heat, running water, and telephones allowed medical personnel to work in a modern environment.

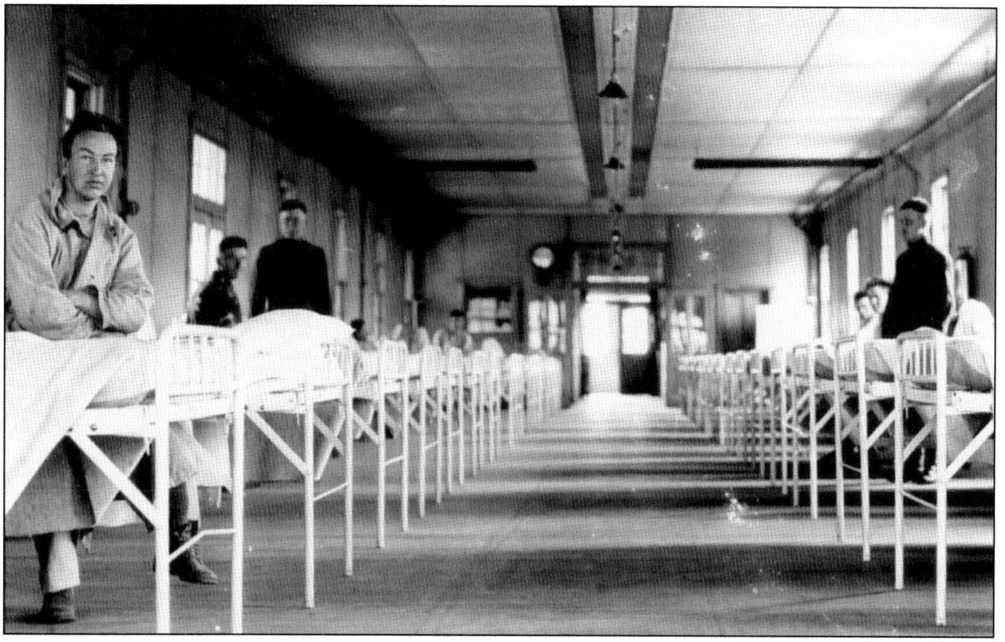

Medical resources were put to their greatest test during the Spanish influenza epidemic in October 1918. By the end of November, Camp Dodge saw 10,008 cases of flu, 1,923 cases of pneumonia, and 702 deaths. The hospital was overwhelmed. Doctors, nurses, and other staff worked continually, and some of them, too, succumbed. Hoping to keep news of the epidemic from reaching the enemy in Germany, the U.S. Army ceased communicating with the outside world. This led to false media reports of wrongdoings by medical staff and mass graves on the post. Subsequent independent investigations have revealed no evidence supporting these stories. Instead stories of the heroism and sacrifices of the medical staff have come to light. The epidemic ran its course, with few cases after November. U.S. Army nurses, making the most of their off duty moments (below), celebrate Christmas with dinner and crepe paper decorations.

When the search for national cantonment locations began, officials from Iowa's capital, Des Moines, decided to join the competition. Patriotism was one incentive, but another was the influx of money that the camp, the soldiers, and their visiting families would bring. Leaders promoted the city, stressing a climate like that of Europe, and a city free from vice. Other area contenders were Fort Snelling, Minnesota, and Cedar Rapids, Iowa.

The Des Moines Coliseum, constructed as both an armory and an auditorium, was the site of many wartime events. Former president William Taft appeared at both Camp Dodge and the coliseum in 1917. Theodore Roosevelt also visited the post and spoke at the coliseum in May 1918. The 200-member Alabama Chorus, formed from African American soldiers in the 366th Infantry, also performed at the coliseum for an audience of over 5,000.

The small communities around the post also provided activities for the soldiers. The small farm-to-market town of Herrold (above) was engulfed by the post's northward expansion and became a popular destination. Other small cities sprang up on the east side of the post. Dodge City and Army City boasted stores, barbers, a theater, and a hotel. To ensure proper hygienic standards, all had to certify that their merchants had the proper licenses and shots.

The Dodge City Hotel, located to the north of the post's massive water reservoir, opened in January 1918. In its first year, the hotel hosted over 10,000 guests, including a number of U.S. Army nurses who were awaiting the completion of their housing on the post. Most of Dodge City was destroyed by fire in 1919. Its southern neighbor, Army City, was located east of the Hyperion Field and Motor Club.

A native of Kenwood, 25-year-old Pvt. Grant D. Wood entered the U.S. Army on September 5, 1918, after waiving his right to an exemption for flatfeet. He served at Camp Dodge with the 163rd Depot Brigade. Utilizing his artistic talents, the U.S. Army later reassigned him to a camouflage unit, Company B, Regiment 97, U.S. Army Engineers, near Washington D. C. He was discharged on December 20, 1918. (Courtesy of the State Historical Society of Iowa, Iowa City.)

Jay C. Hormel, dressed in a privately purchased uniform, became the first Minnesota inductee at Camp Dodge when processed on September 5, 1917, and served with Company C, 351st Infantry, 88th Division. Hormel moved rapidly up the ranks becoming a second lieutenant before departing camp in November 1918. Hormel later pioneered the development of Spam in the mid-1930s. (Courtesy of Hormel Foods.)

George C. Whitmer earned the distinction of being the first man inducted into the U.S. Army at Camp Dodge on September 5, 1917. A resident of Des Moines, Whitmer served with the 88th Division and eventually deployed to Europe with the division in August 1918. He served as mayor of Des Moines from 1966 to 1968 and has a park named for him in east-central Des Moines.

Of German ancestry, Russian-born Marie Jedamus fled with her family from the Ukraine in 1893, settling in Wisconsin. At the onset of World War I, she joined the U.S. Army Nurse Corps and was stationed at Camp Dodge. During the influenza epidemic she never let her family know of the horrors surrounding her. She never married and continued a U.S. Army career until the 1930s, when she returned home to care for her mother. (Courtesy of Douglas Pledger.)

In October 1919, officers and men of the 4th Regiment, Iowa National Guard, enjoy coffee during a cold day at the Camp Dodge rifle range along the flood basin of the Des Moines River, east of then Beaver Road. Following World War I, Iowa undertook the task of rebuilding the Iowa National Guard and recruiting personnel to offset the discharges of many war-weary Iowa National Guard veterans of World War I.

Three

Rebuilding and Growing 1921–1929

After the war, the U.S. Army no longer needed the land or the expensive improvements that had been made to Camp Dodge. Citing the rapid deterioration of the temporary buildings, officials decided not to keep the property as a U.S. Army post. Camp Dodge was on its way to becoming a virtual ghost town.

By 1920, a small contingent of about 600 men remained; their job was to guard the remaining military property and prepare it for shipment to new locations.

The first federal auction of surplus buildings took place in July 1920. Then in May 1921, the Department of War sold much of the remaining building stock to the Northwestern Lumber and Wrecking Company. Northwestern Lumber then conducted its own auctions on-site.

As the U.S. Army prepared to leave, new Iowa governor Nathan Kendall and Adj. Gen. Louis Lasher shared a vision—that of making Camp Dodge into a National Guard training center second to none.

More than 650 of the post's buildings, plus water system improvements, were located on the original National Guard–owned property. The federal government agreed to turn over all improvements on that property in exchange for $35,000. Money then received from salvage operations on the state land would be used to improve the post.

A grand plan for the entire grounds was drawn up by the Des Moines firm of Pearse, Robinson and Sprague. Included in the scheme was a huge swimming pool, a central recreation building, a camp hospital, and regimental housing and infirmaries. The buildings were to be grouped around a quadrangle and designed with a Spanish feel, with long porches and open design. Although the pool's bathing pavilion would be designed like this, the rest of the plan was not to be.

Although annual training took place at Camp Dodge in 1921, the state did not gain full control of the post until March 1922. Camp Dodge continued to be the annual training site for most Iowa National Guard units throughout the 1920s, but changes were coming as a stock market crash and a depression loomed.

These two over-flight photographs show the changes occurring at Camp Dodge as it returned to state ownership. Above is the post during the annual encampment in 1923, looking toward the north. Gone are the deteriorating World War I buildings. Since the improvements and buildings in this area had been sold to the state by the Department of War, the Iowa National Guard was able to auction off the World War I buildings to help fund new construction. Sales from the auction netted $69,000, and new construction was started. To the left is the post around 1926, with the view now looking to the south. The series of brick dining halls on the left had been completed, as well as the barrel-roofed recreation hall. The costs for constructing the 50 mess halls, 3 regimental headquarters buildings, and 11 bathhouses came to $168,000.

After World War I, the Iowa National Guard continued an agreement with the federal government to use the rifle ranges adjacent to Camp Dodge. In 1916, the Iowa National Guard had requested the purchase of enough land to join Camp Dodge with the range. In the center of the photograph, which is looking to the west toward Beaver Road, is one of the homes used to house Camp Dodge employees.

Members of the 168th Infantry gather at the rifle range for target practice in 1924. The targets in the background overlooked the Des Moines River, located to the east. The river was notoriously dangerous and the land was flood-prone. The Des Moines River took the lives of at least five soldiers and camp workers between 1909 and 1921.

The brick North Arsenal (above) was the first military building constructed on the post and dates to 1915–1916. Designed by Frank E. Wetherell, it was "guaranteed fireproof," an important selling point for an arsenal. It was put to the test in January 1922 when a Camp Dodge employee, Charles Kinsey, was cleaning the building. The contents of a bucket, thought to be sawdust and floor sweepings, were thrown into the furnace. In actuality the bucket contained black powder. The explosion threw Kinsey into the air and rocked the building. Adj. Gen. Louis Lasher, who was at the statehouse at the time, hurried to the scene, put the injured man into his automobile, and rushed him to the hospital. Fire crews contained the fire by flooding the basement. The brick South Arsenal (below) located across the street, was built in 1917. These photographs are from around 1934 and 1942.

As part of the post–World War I improvements, a series of 50 company dining halls were constructed on Des Moines Avenue. When Iowa National Guard units attended training at Camp Dodge, the buildings housed the kitchen and provided a dining area for troops. Tents were erected by company in rows directly to the west of each mess hall. Also constructed during 1923 to 1926 were a motor transport building to house National Guard–owned vehicles, three regimental headquarters buildings, nine stables, a blacksmith shop, and a recreation building.

The construction of an outdoor swimming pool and bathing pavilion was announced in July 1921, with completion in 1922. National Guard leaders saw the pool as an asset in their plan to recruit the postwar National Guard to full strength again. The 1920s emphasis on health and fitness meshed with the goals of the National Guard, and the pool would provide an annual training incentive, described to recruits as a "two week vacation." The $87,000 pool's dedication was to feature the Fort Des Moines Army Band. Although Gov. Nathan Kendall was slated to take the first dive into the pool, he was instead called away to assist in negotiations with striking coal miners and railroad workers. Panoramic photographs of the pool in 1922 and 1923 also illustrate the changes taking place on the rest of the post as the World War I buildings were dismantled and new buildings erected.

This 1924 photograph shows the front of the bathing pavilion, featuring its deep porch and Spanish design. The original postwide plan envisioned by the Des Moines firm of Pearse, Robinson and Sprague did not materialize, the proposal abandoned after the pool's construction. The beautifully designed pool complex, however, captured the interest of the entire state. National Guard officials quickly realized that it could be a community asset, especially during the period when the National Guard was not present for annual training. The Des Moines Playground Association, an offshoot of the Rotary Club, was formed to manage the pool. The group continued the pool's operation until its closure in 2002. During the 1920s, area residents could spend the day swimming for the sum of 30¢. It was also the site of a number of Amateur Athletic Union swim meets throughout the 1920s and 1930s.

The 133rd Infantry Band (above) and Troop E of the 1st Cavalry (below) pose in front of remnants of the World War I post. Although annual training took place at Camp Dodge in 1921, the state did not gain full control of the post until March 1922. At the end of the war, over 650 of the buildings, as well as the wells, water tank, and sewer connections, were located on the original Iowa National Guard–owned property. The buildings on this land stayed intact while negotiations took place between Adj. Gen. Louis Lasher and U.S. Army staff. The final agreement stated that for $35,000, the federal government would turn over all improvements located on prewar Camp Dodge lands, including the water works system. Money received from salvage operations on state land would then be used for post improvements.

Two images, one taken in 1921 and the other in 1925, show the changes brought about at Camp Dodge in a few short years. In 1921, Waterloo's Company D, 133rd Infantry, poses in front of the deteriorating World War I barracks with M1917 .30 caliber water-cooled machine guns and mule drawn M1917 machine gun carts. In 1925, Company L, 133rd Infantry soldiers, Sioux City, pose in front of their new mess hall. What has not changed is the appearance of curious soldiers peering out doors and windows.

For a cavalry soldier the ability to maintain his position in the saddle during close combat was of utmost importance. Pictured here are members of Company K, 1st Iowa Cavalry Regiment, during annual training, 1921. The troopers were mounted bareback and engaged in wrestling matches with the goal of removing their opponent from his horse. The activity developed horsemanship, agility, and upper body strength.

Soldiers of the 1st Iowa Cavalry await their turn on the firing line at the Camp Dodge rifle range during annual training in August 1921. The troopers are armed with M1911 .45-caliber automatic pistols carried in leather holsters. Regulations required that all Iowa National Guard troops qualify with their weapons once per year. The man on the right holds a camera. The 1st Iowa Cavalry was renamed the 113th Cavalry Regiment on April 9, 1923.

The spiritual needs of the Iowa National Guard soldiers were not overlooked by supervising officers at annual training. Members of the 133rd Infantry Band, Fairfield, play at a Sunday Camp Dodge field church service as the chaplain, seated, looks on.

Looking to the west, the beautifully landscaped expanse of Camp Dodge and the largest pool in Iowa are evident in this picture of a troop formation of the 113th Cavalry in August 1929.

Annual encampments featured events that demonstrated the abilities of the soldiers. Competitive marksmanship, drilling, and even sporting events were highlights of the two weeks. The public eagerly attended to catch a glimpse of the soldiers and special guests. Governor's Day was an opportunity for the companies to display their skills before their commander-in-chief. The 1923 encampment (above) featured a review of the troops by Gov. Nathan Kendall, seated on the white horse. Kendall, the son of a Civil War veteran, had a special fondness for Camp Dodge and loved to ride his horse Charger on the post. A later photograph (below, from around 1926) shows Gov. John Hammill next to Adj. Gen. Louis Lasher, who was named to the post of adjutant general in 1918 when Gen. Guy Logan resigned to serve in the U.S. Army.

Other encampment highlights included ceremonial reviews by notable public figures. In 1924, the Iowa National Guard was reviewed by Gen. John J. "Black Jack" Pershing, who retired later that year. Pershing was commander of the American Expeditionary Forces in World War I and was later named general of the armies, the first to hold that title since George Washington. In 1929, Tom Mix, movie star and "King of the Cowboys," reviewed the 113th Cavalry. Mix was renowned as one of Theodore Roosevelt's Rough Riders, but some authorities now note that Mix enlisted for the Spanish-American War but went AWOL to marry his fiancée. The U.S. Army belatedly discovered the mistake and his true military record remained a secret until his death in 1940. Mix can be seen below wearing his trademark white cowboy hat. (Below, courtesy of the Iowa City Armory.)

A 1927 visit by a U.S. Army airship gave added excitement to the Iowa National Guard's annual training at Camp Dodge. At 382 feet in length, the RS-1 was the U.S. Army's largest semirigid airship. (By comparison, the *Hindenberg*, which would gain notoriety when it exploded a decade later, was 804 feet in length.) The RS-1's landing required a ground crew of 140 specially trained soldiers from the 168th Infantry. The dirigible also flew low over Des Moines so that residents could view the military aircraft but due to impending thunderstorms, had to quickly depart from Camp Dodge for its home station in Belleville, Illinois.

Four

Surviving the Hard Times 1930–1940

As the Great Depression deepened, the National Guard became an unintended beneficiary of the crisis, at least in the ease of getting new members. Recruiting was at an all-time high. Families needed every dollar possible, and one source of income was drill pay provided by National Guard membership. It was not easy duty, though, and as the farm crisis intensified and labor unrest grew, guardsmen found themselves standing between their neighbors and the enforcement of unpopular laws.

Ammunition and supplies were moved from the Camp Dodge arsenal building in September 1931 as Gov. Dan Turner, himself a former guardsman, declared martial law in Cedar County. Farmers near Tipton had rebelled against the mandatory tuberculin testing of their cattle, fearing the loss of their herds. The National Guard was called up to enforce the testing. While the troops were at their 1932 annual training at Camp Dodge, a farmers' strike was escalating. Des Moines buses were kept on hand should the troops be needed in other parts of the state. In 1938, the 113th Cavalry attended annual training fresh from service in Newton, where martial law was declared to contain the Maytag Washing Machine Company strike.

During the 1930s, several New Deal programs were enacted to provide employment and strengthen the economy, including the 1933 Civilian Conservation Corps (CCC) and the Works Progress Administration (WPA). Adj. Gen. Charles Grahl was given the responsibility of heading the CCC program in Iowa. The WPA also had a headquarters at Camp Dodge.

In 1935, the post hosted the training of the newly formed Iowa Highway Patrol. In 1938, it became the site of Iowa's first American Legion's Hawkeye Boys State.

During the 1930s, the Iowa National Guard became more specialized and the troops, especially the artillery, needed more land on which to train. During the last part of the decade their training did not take place at Camp Dodge. However, the infantry and cavalry continued to train at Camp Dodge through 1939.

As the decade played out and Europe went to war, the Iowa National Guard prepared for possible service. Camp Dodge was to play its part, becoming, once again, part of the U.S. Army.

This aerial photograph, around 1930, looks south and east toward the Des Moines River valley. The swimming pool is at the center left and company dining halls can be seen running diagonally through the center of the photograph along Des Moines Avenue. During this period, the post was essentially divided into three parts, with headquarters buildings and dining halls for each of the regiments, the 168th Infantry, the 133rd Infantry, and the 113th Cavalry. To the center right are a series of cavalry stables and to the north (left) of them are the arsenals. To the west (right) of the break in the line of dining halls is the barrel-roofed recreation hall.

This postcard view looks northwest into Camp Dodge during annual training in about 1935. Set up among the permanent buildings of the camp are the tents used by troops during annual training. Partially visible in the left foreground is a German 15-centimeter M1916 field howitzer brought back as a souvenir after World War I. The weapon was claimed by a scrap drive during World War II.

A c. 1935 photograph shows the Camp Dodge rifle range and its line of targets, located in the Des Moines River valley. This area was part of the 1907 federal land purchase. During the 1930s, while the CCC had a headquarters at Camp Dodge, it expended $25,000 in levee work to protect the northern part of the range from flooding and erosion, building dikes and wing dams.

Along with the CCC, the WPA also had a headquarters at Camp Dodge. Workers stationed at Camp Dodge were responsible for landscaping much of the post, constructing a new concession stand at the swimming pool, and building a prominent stone gate, fence, and guardhouse that transformed the post's main entrance from a simple shack and gate (above) to the now signature view of the post that still exists today. The *c.* 1937 guardhouse and fence complex were designed by William N. Nielsen.

The brick farmhouse once owned by the White family (above) continued to be modified for use by the Iowa National Guard. After World War I, it was a blacksmith shop for a time, but then was remodeled to serve as housing once again. Adj. Gen. Louis Lasher and Adj. Gen. Winfred Bailey used it as their residence, and it also served as a headquarters for the commander and staff of the 34th Division during annual encampments. It also was headquarters for the CCC. Located directly south of the house was the headquarters building, which was also used in the 1930s by the CCC and WPA. These photographs are from around 1938.

Three headquarters buildings, designed by the architectural firm of Andersen and Spooner, were built in 1923. Pictured above is the headquarters of the 133rd Infantry from around 1935. Matching buildings were also constructed for the 168th Infantry and the 113th Cavalry Regiments. The building below, located west of the swimming pool, was also designed by Andersen and Spooner in 1923 but was not constructed until about 1934. It served as the brigade headquarters. All four buildings still stand.

The recreation center, built in 1926, served as a central and shared location for indoor recreational activities. Each regiment also had its own post exchange (PX) building where they could buy treats, souvenirs, and other small items. The regimental exchanges were later replaced by a central Army and Air Force Exchange Service (AAFES) building.

In the mid-1930s, a new concession stand was designed for the pool complex and constructed as a WPA project. William N. Nielsen, who also designed the stone guardhouse and fence, originally envisioned that the same limestone facing covering the guardhouse would also grace the concession building's exterior. However, likely due to cost considerations, the stand was built of block.

A future film star who would become president once kept fit at the Camp Dodge Pool, pictured above around 1935. Then WHO Radio sportscaster Ronald Reagan, pictured below, swam there almost daily during the summers of the mid-1930s. Reagan was a former lifeguard and was described as a "fearless" swimmer, even being unsuccessfully recruited for the 1932 Olympic swim team. There are stories told that he once saved a struggling girl from drowning at Camp Dodge and frequently participated with local youths in a game called "King of the Platform." According to his son, his memories surrounding his love of swimming were his most cherished and enduring in his final years. (Courtesy of WHO Radio, Des Moines.)

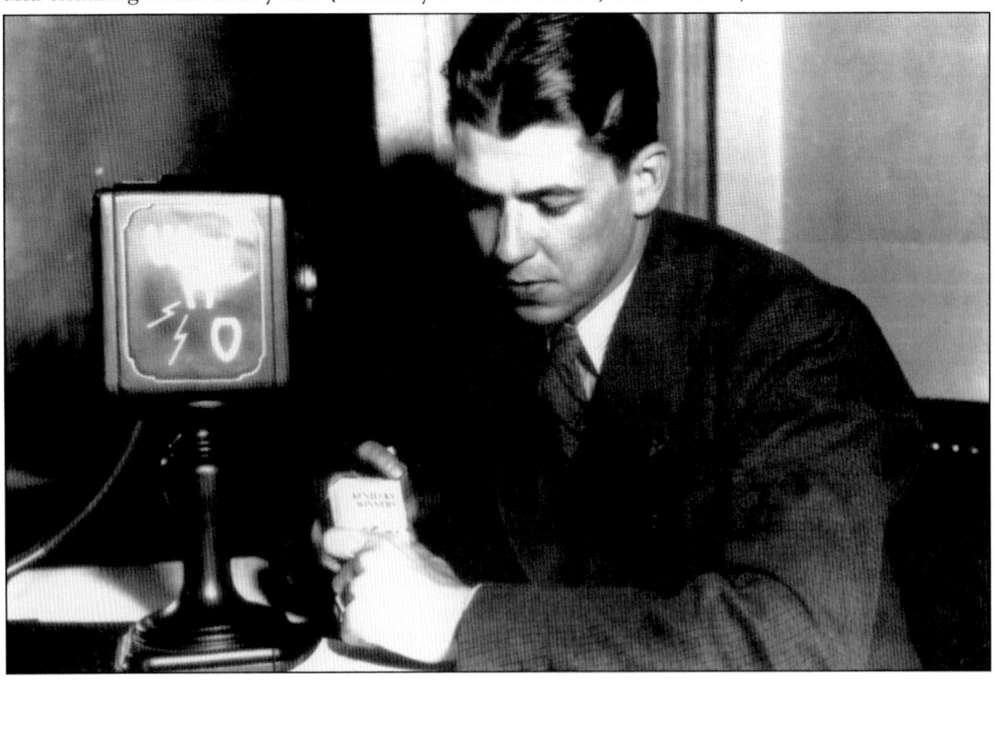

A photograph from a 1938 inventory (above) still shows the temporary wooden roof on the World War I–era storage reservoir. The series of numbers on the right side are part of a gauge that metered the water depth of the tower. The distinctive peaked roof was lost shortly afterwards, as shown in this 1942 photograph (below). While the main body of the tower was constructed of reinforced concrete, it was hastily and cheaply finished with a wooden roof. In the late 1930s, the roof system was failing. Engineering professors at Iowa State University were consulted, and a new framework of steel beams was put in place and a flat roof constructed.

Bids for a Hostess House, designed by Council Bluffs architect William C. Spooner, were advertised in 1930. The building was funded through monies refunded to the National Guard from the federal government and was to be a place where family members could meet while soldiers were at their two-week annual training on the post. It was destroyed by fire in 1957.

A fire in 1931 destroyed two of the post's cavalry stables. More than 80 horses were freed and ran wild through the camp and into Des Moines' residential areas. One source noted that some of the horses were on loan from Fort Des Moines and that several of them managed to make their way safely through Des Moines and back to the fort.

This World War I building, the abandoned Engineer Depot Powderhouse, was photographed for a 1938 inventory. It is one of the last remaining structures built for the 13th National Cantonment. The loading dock to the right opened onto a railroad siding. Located east of the former town of Herrold, the building still stands in the Camp Dodge training area. A twin to the building is located in Camp Shelby, Mississippi, another World War I cantonment.

Pfc. Charlie Sisk (left) and Pfc. Glen Payne, Council Bluffs, with ties neatly tucked between their second and third buttons, polish sabers before an upcoming inspection. Enlisted men did not own sabers, so they are likely working on ones worn by officers in their unit. They sit near the 34th Infantry Division brick farmhouse headquarters building around 1937.

Headquarters Battery and Medical Department Detachment personnel of the 185th Field Artillery pose in front of tractors and towed 155-millimeter howitzers at Camp Dodge in 1930.

Members of the 168th Infantry Band from Council Bluffs are dressed for parade, 1930. This same unit would march into combat in World War II, where the entire band section was captured in February 1943 at the battle of Faid Pass in North Africa.

Radio communications platoon personnel, Headquarters Company, 1st Battalion, 168th Infantry, Des Moines, pose near their radio equipment during annual training in August 1931.

A routine part of annual training each year was passing in review on the Camp Dodge parade ground. With their regimental colors proudly waving in the wind, soldiers of the 136th Medical Regiment, 34th Infantry Division, execute "Column left, march!" in August 1935.

Officers and noncommissioned officers of Company A, 168th Infantry Regiment, Iowa National Guard, Des Moines, pose for a photograph following a 1935 annual training activity called the "Battle of Succotash." The weapons stacked in the background and to the right of the group are M1903 .30 caliber bolt-action rifles. The hat emblems glistening in the sun are the distinctive unit insignia of the 168th Infantry.

The men of Company C, 168th Infantry, Des Moines, pose for their annual training photographs in 1928 (above) and 1935 (below). Two mascots, a young boy and a dog, were with the company in 1928. By 1935, only the dog remained. Mascots, both human and canine, were common among military units through the 1950s. Not-so-common mascots in the Iowa National Guard included a raccoon, a pony named Tiny B, an alligator, a white rooster named Bill, and a bull snake.

In 1935, a four-week instruction period began at Camp Dodge for a new state agency, the Iowa Highway Safety Patrol. The brainchild of Ola Babcock Miller, Iowa's first female secretary of state, the patrol was formed to ensure motorists' safety on the state's highways. In the first year, 85 men trained for 50 open positions. Candidates were given instruction on laws, emergency automobile repairs, first aid, and the use of firearms. Above, Sgt. Wilbur Eicher stands by his 1934 Pontiac patrol car. In the image below, candidates learn motorcycle skills during the second academy in 1937. Officers practiced their skills by patrolling the area around Camp Dodge, returning to the post in the evening. At least one motorcycle has survived and is located at the State Historical Society of Iowa in Des Moines. (Courtesy of the Iowa Highway Patrol section of the Iowa Gold Star Military Museum.)

During annual training around 1938, Iowa National Guard soldiers had the opportunity to inspect one of only three U.S. Army Air Corps Lockheed C-36 cargo aircraft, which had landed at the Camp Dodge airfield. Amelia Earhart piloted a civilian version (Lockheed Electra 10-E) of the C-36 when she disappeared while flying over the Pacific during her unsuccessful 1937 around-the-world trip.

Annual training activities often included the opportunity for guardsmen to familiarize themselves with aircraft and equipment used by other branches of the military. This c. 1938 photograph shows a U.S. Navy Loening OL-9 observation seaplane under examination by curious soldiers.

The 1939 annual encampment was slated to be the last for Maj. Gen. Mathew Tinley, a Council Bluffs native and long-time pillar of the Iowa National Guard. In his over 45 years with the National Guard, Tinley had seen service in the Spanish-American War and as commander of the 168th Infantry Regiment, 42nd Rainbow Division, in World War I. Between wars, he continued his career as a medical doctor. After World War I, he led the reorganization of the 168th Infantry, and in 1924, he was unanimously selected as the commander of the entire 34th Division, a position he held until his retirement. "Dr. Mat," as his friends called him, would again be called to serve his state in World War II. Tinley attended 34th Division events well into the 1950s, sometimes reviewing "his troops" from a wheelchair. He passed away in 1956, a week after his 80th birthday.

Five

The World War II Years 1940–1945

As the country readied for entry into another world war, National Guard soldiers were in the forefront of preparations. The National Guard was ordered phased into active military service starting in September 1940, with Iowa's 34th Infantry Division mobilized in February 1941. In December, as the soldiers made ready for their return from Camp Claiborne, Louisiana, the Japanese attacked Pearl Harbor, drawing the United States into World War II.

Activities such as the annual Hawkeye Boys State and Iowa State Pistol Tournaments were relocated in 1941 in anticipation of Camp Dodge becoming an active U.S. Army facility.

In July, the mayor of Des Moines asked the federal government to locate a bomber plant, an airplane depot, and a cantonment in the area. In September, Adj. Gen. Charles Grahl went to Washington to promote Camp Dodge as a U.S. Army induction center but was not successful. However, in 1942, Camp Dodge was again considered when the induction facility located at Fort Des Moines was moved so that the fort could be used by the Women's Army Auxiliary Corps. In May, a lease transferred portions of Camp Dodge to the U.S. Army for the duration of the war plus six months.

Camp Dodge would not grow as large as in its World War I years, but it was a hub of activity for more than 120,000 recruits. As part of the Armed Forces Induction Station 3722 of the 7th Service Command, new buildings were constructed and old buildings were remodeled. The southern section of the post was reserved for continued state use. The 1st Military Police Battalion was also stationed there as the post's permanent military presence.

In 1944, federal induction centers began to consolidate and close. Camp Dodge was deactivated. The federally leased portion returned to the state, which gained $1 million in improvements. In September, much to the consternation of the National Guard, the federal government also declared the federal land adjacent to Camp Dodge as surplus. An appeal was made so that the National Guard could continue to use the land for training and the sale was halted.

With the war in Europe ending in May 1945, and victory over Japan achieved in August, veterans returned home, anxious to resume and improve their lives.

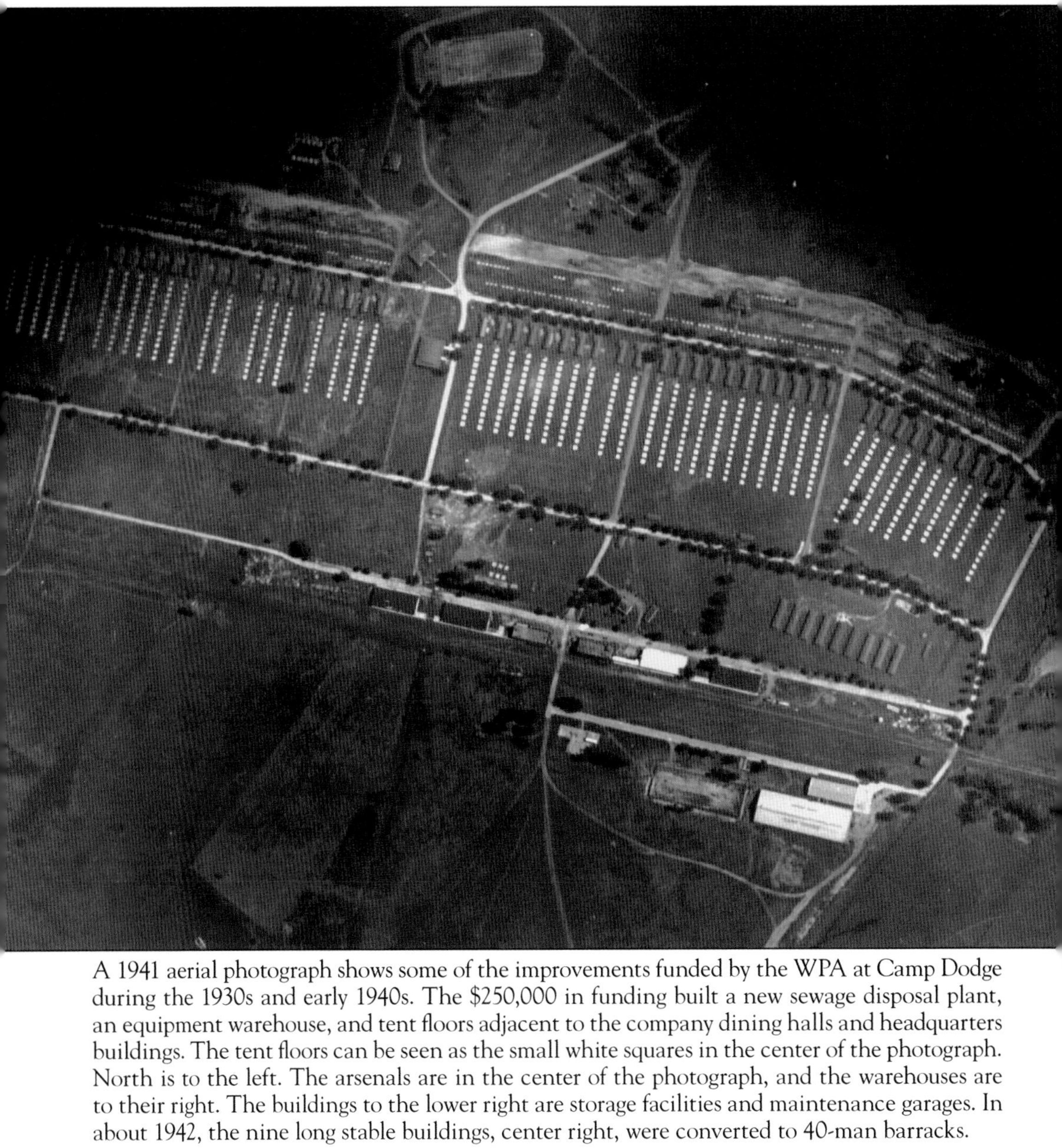

A 1941 aerial photograph shows some of the improvements funded by the WPA at Camp Dodge during the 1930s and early 1940s. The $250,000 in funding built a new sewage disposal plant, an equipment warehouse, and tent floors adjacent to the company dining halls and headquarters buildings. The tent floors can be seen as the small white squares in the center of the photograph. North is to the left. The arsenals are in the center of the photograph, and the warehouses are to their right. The buildings to the lower right are storage facilities and maintenance garages. In about 1942, the nine long stable buildings, center right, were converted to 40-man barracks.

A sentry is stationed at the main gate in this 1940s-era postcard. The building to the right behind the guardhouse is the infirmary, built in 1936. Note also the World War I–era brick-paved road in the foreground.

A 1942 inventory photograph, taken to document Camp Dodge buildings for the transfer from the state to the federal government, shows the pool and bathing pavilion. Observant viewers may note that the pavilion now only has four dormers instead of its original seven. A fire in the late 1930s damaged the roof, and the four salvaged dormers were repositioned.

"Company Street" in this World War II–era postcard is actually Des Moines Avenue, a name it was given in World War I. The company dining halls (now the B-Series Buildings) sport white flower boxes at the front. American elm trees lined both sides of the street. All would succumb to Dutch elm disease in the 1970s. To the rear of the buildings (below) new tent pads, poured around 1941, dot the parade fields. Funded by the WPA, 549 large pads were placed throughout the post, along with 160 small ones. Only a few remain today. The concrete structure between the first two buildings is a coal bin.

One building in the B-Series is not like the others. Building B-61, built in 1934 as the "Mess Hall for the 67th Infantry Brigade," is located to the south of the recreation hall in the center of the row of company dining halls. In 1942, it was updated to an administration building and post office. The tall chimney was connected to the building's stove.

The brick farmhouse was updated as a headquarters building in 1935. In 1945, Gov. Robert Blue spent the summer in a house at Camp Dodge, likely this one. The governor and his family definitely lived here in 1948 during the last six months of his term. Blue had sold his personal residence and the governor's mansion at 2900 Grand Avenue had just been purchased and was in the process of being remodeled.

In May 1940, architect George A. Spooner designed a "Dining Hall and Assembly Building for the Iowa National Guard." The building, located to the west of the brick farmhouse, was then updated by the federal government in 1942 as an officers' mess hall. A pair of light fixtures fashioned from World War I German Mauser rifles and bayonets hang in the west room. A greenhouse was attached to the building from the 1950s through 1980.

Also updated as part of the reception center was the recreation hall, built in 1926. During World War II, it was renamed the Service Club and provided a place for soldiers to socialize. As part of the induction center, the federal government constructed a new theater building west of the Service Club. Both buildings still stand and are now part of the Midwest Counter Drug Training Center.

The Service Club was a commonly visited area during off-duty hours at the Camp Dodge Induction Center. Complimenting the aesthetics were eight 4-by-20-foot murals, two painted at Drake University and six at the University of Iowa, sponsored by Mrs. Edwin T. Meredith of Des Moines. Mrs. Meredith was the widow of the founder of the Meredith Corporation, parent company of *Successful Farming* and *Better Homes and Gardens* magazines. The murals, hung in April 1943 and visible in the upper right of the photograph above, depicted American determination in prior wars and the eventual world triumph over Nazi fascism. Unfortunately only two bas-reliefs (one seen below) are all that remain of the Service Club artwork today.

As the use of trucks and tanks increased in the military, the day of the horse soldier was passing. Nowhere was this better illustrated than at a memorial service held at Camp Dodge in March 1941. Adj. Gen. Charles Grahl, second from the left, prepared to spread a portion of the ashes of Lt. Col. F. D. Couden on the post's parade field. Couden, a cavalry officer from Seattle, Washington, specified in his will that his ashes be divided and spread over six National Guard campgrounds that were part of the 24th Cavalry Division, of which the 113th Cavalry was a part. He expressed the wish "that the horse soldiers of the 24th Cavalry may ride them into the ground." He could not know that there would be no horse soldiers left at his passing, but his ashes now lay where those cavalrymen once rode.

When the war began, Iowa National Guard soldiers were already mobilized, and Iowa had no military presence to protect the state. Veteran Iowa guardsman Lt. Gen. Mathew Tinley (above, right) was asked to come out of retirement and serve as commander of the newly formed Iowa State Guard. The Iowa State Guard was organized in December 1941 and saw service through 1947. Units were stationed throughout the state, normally using the same armories as the prewar National Guard companies. In 1942, all units were put through an intensive 13-week basic training at Camp Dodge, with an annual training period each year until war's end. Pictured below is Company E, 1st Regiment. Emphasizing the importance of a qualified militia presence in the state during wartime, the Iowa State Guard was part of the state's longest civil disturbance call-up, the 92-day Eldora Boys' School riots.

Existing buildings were pressed into service as part of the induction station and reception center. This complex, consisting of a garage, a transportation building, and a truck storage building, was chosen because of its proximity to the Inter-Urban Railway and the large building sizes. The building in the foreground (above) was constructed in 1942 as a WPA project. It was almost immediately put to use by the federal government for soldier processing and clothing issue. Below, in a picture taken as part of a photograph series, one can see "men on the way to the theatre to see sex hygiene and training films." The buildings are now part of the National Maintenance Training Center complex.

As part of the induction and reception center, the federal government built a hospital complex (above) just north of existing state-owned land. Commanding officer Lt. Col. Donald Wilson oversaw a staff of 5 doctors, 94 enlisted men, and 6 nurses. The hospital had a dental office, operating room, three 34-bed wards, complete X-ray service, a medical supply building, and a garage for two ambulances. The original infirmary, located just west of Beaver Road (below) and built in 1936, was also pressed into service as a "special unit" for those soldiers who had not taken their sexual hygiene classes to heart.

Seen to the left, an officer conducts the swearing-in ceremony for new inductees. By the end of the day, their civilian life behind them for the duration of the war, these new citizen-soldiers would become a part of the vast machinery of national defense. Below, after a daylong battery of medical and psychological examinations, aptitude tests, paperwork, and clothing allotments, each man stood before the same mirror dressed in his country's uniform to view "the finest soldier in the world." The mirror and sign would later be used at the Iowa Military Academy.

The company dayroom (above) afforded soldiers the place to relax, read, play cards, write home, and spend their off-duty hours. Although the majority of soldiers inducted at Camp Dodge traveled to other bases for basic training, 4,000 Class I-B "limited service" inductees underwent several weeks of basic training on the post after November 1943. In addition, Iowa State Guard enlistees underwent a shortened basic training program. In the image below, soldiers equipped with cartridge belts and M1 steel helmets, practice a bayonet lunge using .30-caliber Springfield bolt-action rifles.

A U.S. Army band plays as soldiers leave Camp Dodge with their duffle bags packed. The main form of transportation in and out of Camp Dodge was still the electric Inter-Urban Railway. The rail line did not convert to diesel engines until 1949. In 1968, the line was purchased by the Chicago and Northwestern Railroad. The route from Camp Dodge north to Granger was abandoned in 1980, and the rails were torn out shortly after.

Six

Rebuilding with New Missions 1946–1963

As World War II ended, Camp Dodge would again find new missions with the dawn of the Cold War. As 1946 began, the Iowa State Guard met for its final annual training, vowing to stay in top form until the postwar Iowa National Guard could be formed to replace them. Also in 1946, activities such as Hawkeye Boys State and Iowa Highway Patrol training returned to the post.

Iowa National Guard officials gathered to discuss the future structure and the locations of the postwar units. As the National Guard units came back on line, the Iowa State Guard units deactivated, starting in February 1947 and ending that September. In addition, delays in building new armories throughout the state caused an influx of federal vehicles and equipment coming to Camp Dodge warehouses awaiting stationing.

Meanwhile, returning soldiers were flooding college communities, seeking to improve their lives through education paid for by the 1944 G.I. Bill. The state's colleges looked to Camp Dodge to provide housing and classrooms.

In 1948, the federally owned World War II hospital complex was used as a temporary home for patients of the Iowa Lutheran Home for the Aged in nearby Madrid, when the home burned to the ground in January. The post also provided temporary classrooms for the Johnston schools starting in September. That same year, tragedy struck when two Camp Dodge mechanics, flying in a small surplus U.S. Army training plane, crashed on the post, killing both occupants.

The 1950s brought new tenants to Camp Dodge, including the state liquor warehouse and the Iowa Military Academy (IMA). It also became the summer training camp for the Drake University Bulldog football team. The Iowa Air National Guard, formed in 1941, with its headquarters at the Des Moines Airport, also started conducting some of its annual training activities at Camp Dodge.

Another plane crash in 1961 ended less tragically. A wind gust caught a single-engine U.S. Army plane as it attempted to land at Camp Dodge. The plane crashed into a small brick ammunition storage building, injuring the pilot and his passenger.

In 1963, the nation reeled in shock at the assassination of their president, John F. Kennedy. With a new year and a new leader, 1964 signaled more changes ahead.

The 1959 aerial view (above) looks to the west and north. The empty swimming pool is in the forefront, while the B-Series mess halls are hidden by the trees along Des Moines Avenue. The large building in the center is the state liquor warehouse, built around 1954. The elongated building just to the west of the headquarters building and the pool is the new adjutant general's office, completed in 1958. The 1960 view below looks to the east from the pool and shows the Des Moines River valley before the construction of Saylorville Reservoir, a flood control project that would change Camp Dodge's boundaries.

The normally sedate front entrance was transformed for a December 1963 picture. During the 1960s and well into the 1970s, the post was decorated with holiday greetings and lighting displays. Seen below, even the IMA joined in the festivities with Santa sporting a helmet. IMA, founded in 1957, is now known as the 185th Regiment, Regional Training Institute (RTI). The holiday artwork was created by Camp Dodge employee Roger Farris.

The pool continued as a center of community activity. In 1946, however, during the height of the infantile paralysis (polio) scare, a prank call from someone representing themselves as from the State Department of Health forced a one-day closure of the pool. In 1959 to 1960, a massive rehabilitation of the pool resulted in the installation of a filter system and a new concrete pool interior and surrounding deck. In the days before air conditioning was common, there was nothing more appealing than a pool on a hot summer day. Cars and bathers dot the hillside in the *c.* 1960s photograph below.

A longtime tenant of Camp Dodge was the Camp Moingona Girl Scout Camp. A 1940s-inventory photograph shows their lodge. The camp was located on the east side of the post near the Des Moines River and the rifle ranges. With the construction of the Saylorville dam and reservoir the Girl Scouts relocated. Their lodge, however, survives and is used by the U.S. Army Corps of Engineers.

Permanent tent floors mark the site of the Squaw Camp, named in an era when the negative connotations of the word were not recognized. The campsite was used by the wives of soldiers at annual training and was located on current Beaver Drive south of the water reservoir. Members of the Squaw Camp assisted visitors and conducted tours of the post.

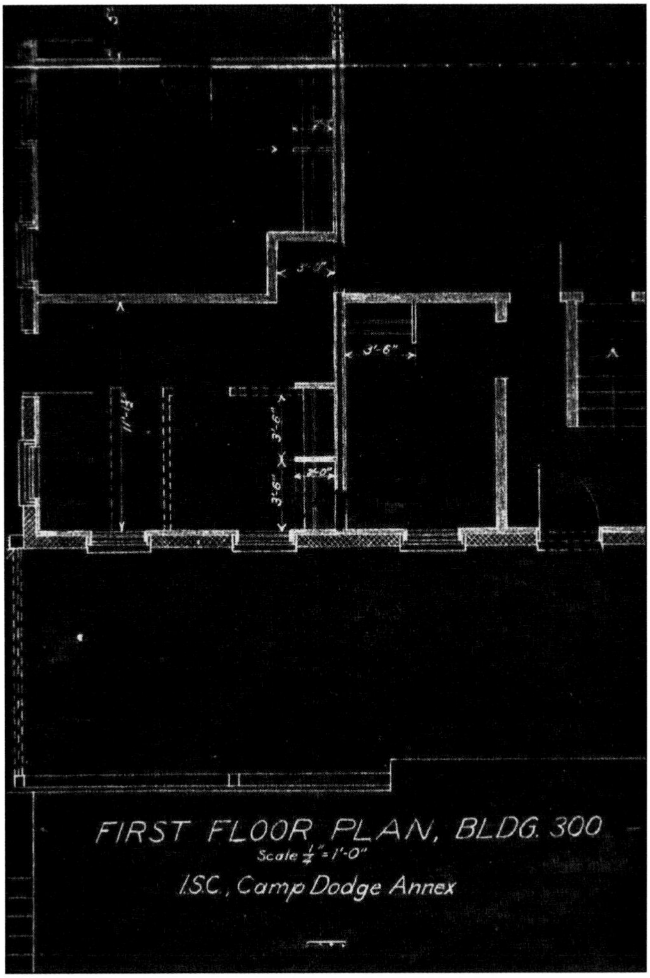

At the end of the war, overwhelmed by returning veterans, Ames's Iowa State College (now University) sought alternate housing and classroom locations. Camp Dodge was suggested as a potential site, and by August 1946, the post was readied for up to 750 male freshmen engineering students. Classes, under the direction of J. P. McKean, would be held only during the normal school year, with the post reserved in the summer for Iowa National Guard training. A number of buildings on the post were updated to accommodate laboratories, classrooms, and dormitories. The Hostess House (below) was turned into an administration building, and the 168th Infantry and 133rd Infantry mess halls and headquarters buildings (plans at left) were used for classrooms and housing. In addition, 250 students were housed at the World War II hospital complex. As class sizes began to diminish, the annex was closed in 1947.

The IMA was founded in 1957 to provide officer candidate and noncommissioned officer training schools, as well as other specialty training classes. Classes were held in the World War II hospital complex, now known as the M-Series. Brig. Gen. Gerald E. DuBois (at right), who had served as the 34th Division artillery commander, was the first IMA commandant. DuBois's career was cut short by his untimely death in 1958 at the age of 56. That same year, a memorial stone was placed on the parade field south of the academy, officially naming it DuBois Field. The memorial rests on one of the few 1940s concrete tent pads left on the post. Pictured by the memorial are, from left to right, Lt. Donald Mueller; Dubois's sons, Jerry and Duane; his widow, Leone; unidentified; Adj. Gen. Fred Tandy; new IMA commandant Frank Williams; and artillery chaplain Edward Ingersoll.

The May 1961 crash of a U.S. Army U1 Otter aircraft at Camp Dodge, while not fatal to pilot or passenger, ended the military flying career of Iowa National Guard pilot Milford Juhl. The plane, piloted by a U.S. Army advisor, was caught by a gust of wind while landing on the parade ground. Juhl, the only passenger, suffered a broken leg and knee injuries. A World War II veteran and accomplished helicopter pilot, Juhl conducted a dramatic air rescue of two stranded boaters near Cedar Rapids in 1959.

The flag at Camp Dodge flies at half-staff on November 24, 1963, two days after the assassination of Pres. John F. Kennedy.

A soldier prepares to fire an M1 carbine at the Camp Dodge range. The construction of a flood control project, creating Saylorville Reservoir, would soon flood the range, used since 1906. The firing ranges were relocated to their current location east of nearby Beaver Creek in the mid-1960s through the mid-1970s.

Marking and replacing targets was an integral part of range firings. A soldier stands in a protective trench and waves a red flag known as "Maggie's drawers" to indicate that a shooter on the firing line has missed the target. The slang term for the flag is believed to be based on a bawdy drinking song, "Those Old Red Flannel Drawers that Maggie Wore."

Brig. Gen. Charles Grahl was adjutant general from 1932 until 1950, the longest appointment ever. The World War I veteran saw his troops prepare for World War II, served as the state's Selective Service director, and guided the reorganization of the Iowa National Guard after World War II. He left in 1950 to accept a position with the U.S. Army's Selective Service division.

Although some governors had been National Guardsmen previous to their election, only one, Lt. Col. Norman Erbe, was a guardsman while governor. A decorated World War II B-17 pilot, Erbe served as Boone County attorney and Iowa attorney general before his election as governor (1961–1963). In 1962 he spent his annual training period as an instructor at IMA. (Courtesy of the Iowa National Guard Records Center.)

Seven

THE VIETNAM ERA 1964–1975

The Vietnam War era was a time when emotions ran high. As demonstrations occurred against the war throughout the country, many protestors included the National Guard in their antiwar activities. Although two Iowa National Guard units were called up for service in Vietnam, Camp Dodge was not used as a deployment site.

Changes were coming to Camp Dodge's historic boundaries, as the Army Corps of Engineers began a flood control project on the Des Moines River. The project was envisioned in 1940 but did not see funding until the 1960s. The massive Saylorville Dam project, with groundbreaking in 1965, flooded 26,000 acres of the valley, including the post's shooting ranges, wells, and five homes used for employee housing.

Also in 1965, due to the threat of demonstrations and riots at the Iowa State Fair, troops from the 168th Infantry were called-up to keep order. Although the fairgrounds stayed quiet, troops from the 168th Infantry practiced riot control dills at Camp Dodge while serving as backup for the 186th Military Police, who normally assisted with fair crowd control.

Even proposed new construction created controversy, as a law enforcement academy building and a chapel were planned. The legality of building a nonmilitary building on Camp Dodge was questioned, as well as the construction of a religious structure on government-owned ground.

The post continued to host the liquor warehouse, the Drake University football team's summer practice, and events such as sporting dog trials. It also again provided temporary classrooms for Johnston schools.

Other signs of the times were a 1966 shortage of fatigues for Iowa guardsmen (due to priority needs in Vietnam) and a 1973 U.S. Army ruling that guardsmen could wear wigs to drill so that their hair would meet the shorter military standards. The 1973 gas shortage resulted in orders limiting military vehicle use to mission-essential purposes.

In 1972, Adj. Gen. Joseph May swore in Mary Ketchum, the first female member of the Iowa Army National Guard.

As the Vietnam War came to a close, Camp Dodge was an arrival point for Vietnam refugees, part of Gov. Robert Ray's Indochinese Resettlement Task Force.

In the mid-1960s, the Saylorville flood control project began to inundate the post's ranges and homes used by Camp Dodge employees. In the image above, Rep. Neal Smith, at podium, speaks at the project's groundbreaking on July 17, 1965, while Gov. Robert Ray and military officials look on. Below, a 1940s inventory photograph shows one of the Camp Dodge residences lost to Saylorville Dam's construction. Part of the land agreement for the creation of the dam included the construction of new homes on Camp Dodge proper to replace those lost to the project. On-post residences were normally occupied by civilian state employees, who were caretakers and maintenance personnel. Civilian employees were a mainstay from the start, caring for the post even when the military was not present.

The Camp Dodge pool continued to draw thousands of swimmers each year. The grassy hill on the east side of the pool provided an ideal spot for parents watching children and for girl-watchers enjoying the latest in swimsuit fashion. In 1974, the pool was opened to the participants of the Des Moines Register's Annual Great Bike Ride Across Iowa (RAGBRAI) as they passed through central Iowa. In 1975, a tragic accident took the life of 21-year-old Sherwood Wallace, one of a number of people who lost their lives at the pool throughout the years.

By the 1970s, the brick farmhouse had been remodeled several times and served as the permanent home of the adjutant general. This 1967 winter photograph shows the continuing tradition of holiday decorations, with a giant greeting card in the yard. During a 1969 remodel, the entire exterior of the house was painted white.

The adjutant general's headquarters building was also decorated for the season. Constructed in 1958, the building allowed the adjutant general to move his main office from the State Capitol, 10 miles away, to Camp Dodge, now the center of Iowa National Guard activity. In addition, a small office was maintained at the statehouse.

After four years of legislative and legal discussions, the Camp Dodge Memorial Building was funded as a memorial building rather than as a chapel. On May 31, 1971, Gov. Robert Ray spoke at the dedication ceremony. The building would also become the first home of the Iowa Gold Star Military Museum. In the 1987 photograph (above), visitors await the formal dedication of the 34th Infantry Division Memorial. On September 12, the memorial was dedicated to the memory of all soldiers who served with or were attached to the 34th Infantry Division during combat in North Africa and Italy during World War II. The memorial lists all the battles fought by the division, the days of combat, and awards presented to division soldiers.

IMA first-year plebes pass in review (above). Several Camp Dodge landmarks can be seen in the background, with one of the original farmhouses between the flags and the South Arsenal (Building W-5) to the right. Seen below dressed in summer khaki uniforms, pistol belts, and glossy helmet liners, IMA senior cadets express their appreciation for off-post visitors during their final weeks of Officer Candidate School. White helmets were worn by the plebes/candidates, and black helmets were reserved for senior cadets.

IMA candidates "stack arms" during Officer Candidate School training. The mid-1960s saw longtime IMA proponent, Lt. Col. Eric P. Berner, promoted to academy commandant and also saw the first African American candidate, Robert Randle of Des Moines.

An IMA cadet, dressed in starched olive green fatigues and Ridgeway field cap, receives marksmanship instruction on the use of the .30-caliber M1 Garand rifle.

A letter from General of the Army Omar Bradley was to be the first article placed in the Camp Dodge Memorial Building archives. In the letter, sent to Adj. Gen. Joseph May, Bradley reflected on his duty as a major with the 19th Infantry Division at Camp Dodge during World War I. The Missouri native did not see combat and at the time feared his military career was over. He also recalled losing some of his closest friends during the 1918 influenza epidemic. Known as "the soldier's general," Bradley rose to fame in World War II for his combat leadership. After the war, he headed the Veteran's Administration and was later named chairman of the Joint Chiefs of Staff. He died in 1981 and was the U.S. Army's last five-star general.

Eight

A Resource for the Soldier and the Community 1976–1989

The post-Vietnam years continued with changes in American society that were reflected at Camp Dodge as well. The role of women was shifting as they were directly integrated into the United States military. In 1976, the first four women attended Officer Candidate School at the IMA. A year later, 2nd Lt. Joyce Naughton, Army Reserve, was the first to graduate.

Under the increased scrutiny of the press, irregularities in the leadership at Camp Dodge were reported. Two adjutant generals became enmeshed in scandals, and Camp Dodge became the center of charge and counter-charge. Gen. Joseph May was accused of inappropriate use of government aircraft, leading to his removal. His successor, Gen. Junior Burkhead, was also accused of improper use of government resources. Employees were torn into factions and Burkhead resigned.

In 1977, as part of a recruiting event for high school students called "Guardsman for a Day," an officer was reprimanded for allowing under-age drinking during an overnight visit to Camp Dodge. Some of the boys obtained beer and smuggled it into camp. They then became rowdy, broke a car windshield, and entered a women's barracks.

The news was not all bad, however, and in 1977, a new armory on the post was dedicated in honor of former adjutant general Junior Miller, who served as adjutant general from 1961 to 1969. The final phase of the Iowa Law Enforcement Academy (ILEA) was dedicated. Present for the event were Gov. Robert Ray and FBI Director Clarence M. Kelley.

More Vietnamese refugees were welcomed at Camp Dodge in 1979. In the same year, under the supervision of Col. (later brigadier general) Harold Thompson, Camp Dodge became the staging point and support base for the October visit of Pope John Paul II to nearby Living History Farms.

The post's long history was finally recognized with a museum. The brainchild of Col. Aloysius Rolfes and Brig. Gen. Edward Bird, the museum was first located in the lower floor of the Camp Dodge Memorial Building, with its grand opening in June 1985.

As the 1980s ended, after almost 22 years without a call-up for federal service, the fate of the Iowa National Guard was about to change.

An April 1980 photograph captures part of Camp Dodge, with the Saylorville Reservoir's emergency spillway located on the top right. To the right of the pool (center right) is the Camp Dodge Memorial Building and its parking lot, built in 1971. At the bottom center of the photograph, just above the B-Series mess halls, is the ILEA, completed in 1977. The large building at the bottom right is the State Liquor Warehouse, which was transferred to the Iowa National Guard in 1981 and now used as the U.S. Property and Fiscal Office Warehouse. North is to the left.

Members of the 1980 American Legion Hawkeye Boys State gather for a group photograph in the shape of the state of Iowa. With the exception of World War II, Boys State has been held annually at Camp Dodge since 1938. The building to the rear was used as an officers' mess hall in World War II, then became the officers' club. It was later renamed the Dodge House and is still used for various training and social events.

In September 1985, Camp Dodge held its first Command Retreat. The event was the initiative of Adj. Gen. Warren G. Lawson and recognized achievements of both Iowa National Guard soldiers and civilians. A month later, Lawson's brother, U.S. Air Force Lt. Gen. Richard A. Lawson, deputy commander, Chief United States European Command, officiated at a second Command Retreat in front of the adjutant general's headquarters.

The Iowa Gold Star Military Museum, under the direction of Col. (retired) Aloysius T. Rolfes, was founded at Camp Dodge in June 1985. Building on a collection of historic items formerly on exhibit at IMA, the Iowa National Guard Memorial Commission consolidated those items and others located throughout the post. They were then placed in a museum facility located on the ground floor of the Camp Dodge Memorial Building.

National Guard veteran Brig. Gen. (retired) Edward W. Bird (left), Adj. Gen. Warren G. Lawson, and museum director Col. (retired) Aloysius T. Rolfes, pose with donations to the museum in July 1988. Bird and Rolfes, combat veterans of World War II, worked together to establish the museum as an educational component of the Iowa National Guard Memorial Commission.

Historically the Des Moines National Guard units had been scattered in various locations throughout the city. In 1977, an armory on Camp Dodge was constructed for their use. Named Junior Miller Armory in honor of former adjutant general Junior Miller, the building was dedicated on July 7, 1977. Maj. Gen. Junior Miller (below, right) retired in 1969 after eight years as adjutant general. Miller served 42 years in the National Guard and was a veteran of World War II.

The dedication of the completion of the ILEA took place in May 1977. The first phase of the project was dedicated in 1969, while the second phase, which included classrooms and dormitory facilities, was completed in the mid-1970s. The academy, an independent state agency, provides training and certification to Iowa law enforcement officers.

The 1977 IMA graduation, the academy's 20th, included the first woman to complete the program. Although four women began the course in 1976, only 2nd Lt. Joyce Naughton (far left, first row), completed the rigorous training. Naughton, a resident of Cedar Rapids, commuted to Camp Dodge on weekends and for annual training, while maintaining her job as a junior high school teacher during the week. (Courtesy of the 185th Regiment, Regional Training Institute.)

Nine

Training Center for Global War Fighting 1990–2009

The last decade of the 20th century brought a world of change to Camp Dodge. An invasion by Iraqi dictator Saddam Hussein into a little-known country called Kuwait initiated the National Guard into full partnership with the full-time regular military. The first call-up of Iowa National Guard soldiers began in September 1990. More than 1,700 would be deployed.

Negotiations were underway with neighboring landowners as Camp Dodge sought to expand after losing over 500 acres to the Saylorville Dam project. The post would eventually grow by an additional 2,000 acres. The small town of Herrold would also be drawn into the post's borders.

The State Area Readiness Command (STARC) Armory was constructed between Saylorville and Camp Dodge proper. Hailed as "the armory of the future," it housed a self-contained State Emergency Operations Center (SEOC). The new Iowa Communications Network connected Iowa National Guard facilities statewide as part of its fiber-optic system.

Record flooding in 1993 found Camp Dodge as the staging area for statewide relief efforts. When Des Moines lost its water plant, the post, with its own water supply, became a refuge for those without water. In 1998, Camp Dodge found itself needing "rescue," when a mesocyclone, packing 120-mile-an-hour winds, tore through the post.

On a September morning in 2001, a strange story began to pass through the post—an airplane had crashed into a building in New York City. Within minutes, reports confirmed that the improbable rumor was a horrible reality. Worries increased when it was realized that some Camp Dodge employees were en route by plane to Washington, D. C.

The post went under a security lockdown, and Camp Dodge would never be the same again. The days of unrestricted access ended. The post saw farewell ceremonies and homecomings as Iowa National Guard soldiers left for service in Iraq, Afghanistan, and other theaters of operation in the War on Terror.

Since then, the post has seen new construction and new training areas, allowing soldiers to train for terrorist threats. Well-known landmarks were also lost or closed, including the World War I water reservoir and the Camp Dodge pool.

This June 1993 photograph looks east toward Saylorville Reservoir. In the forefront is the Camp Dodge range complex, moved in the mid-1960s from the Des Moines River valley to make way for the flood control project's dam, seen at top center. An entire series of maintenance buildings, located in the center of the photograph, provide repair sites for military vehicles and equipment. The open fields to the right are now filled with military classrooms, office buildings, housing, and mess halls. Just below the dam is an open construction site, future home of the STARC Armory, pictured below after its completion in 1994. The building, now known as the Joint Forces Headquarters, houses many of the Iowa National Guard's administrative offices, including the office of the adjutant general. It was designed by Sires Architects of Johnston.

Changing security requirements and an increased traffic flow created the need for a new main entrance for Camp Dodge. The old main gate, with its stone guardhouse, was closed to general traffic and a modern entrance, complete with security building, was constructed on Northwest Seventieth Avenue. Inspection of incoming vehicles has become an additional responsibility of the post's state security personnel. In the background of this 2009 photograph are buildings making up the post's battalion housing complex, as well as the 734th Maintenance Battalion Armory. To the northwest of the new entrance is the Iowa Army National Guard Freedom Center (below), completed in 2008. It serves as a readiness center for a number of Iowa National Guard units. It also houses classrooms for Grandview College's Johnston campus. Grandview College has offered accelerated degree program classes at the post for many years.

Old landmarks remained as the centennial year of 2009 began. The White family's 1873 brick house served as the traditional adjutants general's residence until 2005. The home was undergoing renovations in early 2009. Once completed, it will again be the adjutant general's residence. Below, an M48 Patton tank, a longtime resident of the Beaver Drive tank park display area, still stands guard over the Beaver Creek valley. Security requirements, caused by the September 11, 2001, terrorist attacks, forced the fencing of the hillside, which had long been a popular winter sledding spot.

The North Arsenal, Camp Dodge's first military building, is now designated building W-6 and houses the logistics branch of the Camp Dodge training site management section. The WPA-era stone guardhouse entrance on Beaver Drive still stands, but as seen in this 2009 photograph, it is no longer a public entrance to the post.

During the 1990s, negotiations began with neighboring landowners for the purchase of additional training land. The new property, much of it formerly in agricultural row-crop production, required a quick transformation into land capable of training soldiers. In addition, the new acquisition contained areas of fragile wetlands and woodlands that required protection. Partnerships were formed with area colleges and other government agencies in order to study and manage the sites. In the image above, Camp Dodge personnel inspect a pothole wetland. In the scene below, as part of a Boy Scout field day, an Iowa State University staffer leads a wetland tour.

A weather event called a mesocyclone bore down on Camp Dodge in the early afternoon of Monday, June 29, 1998. Straight-line winds of over 120 miles per hour downed decades-old trees and damaged 187 of the post's 235 buildings. Although damages were set at over $6.6 million, none of the post's employees was seriously injured in the storm. The Dodge House (above), lost its porch and the roof on the west side of the building. In the image below, Seventh Street, south of the Camp Dodge Memorial Building, was blocked by the fall of one of the large trademark cottonwood trees that stand throughout the post.

In September 2007, the sound of a wrecking ball echoed through Camp Dodge. A longtime landmark, the Camp Dodge water tower was destroyed, replaced by a modern one. Technically built as a water reservoir, it had been in continuous service since its construction in World War I, serving as the main water storage site for Camp Dodge's water system. Located on the ridge between the Des Moines River and Beaver Creek, the distinctive structure provided a navigational landmark in many historic Camp Dodge pictures.

On the morning of September 12, 2007, the water reservoir still stood next to the new Camp Dodge water tower (left) and the city of Johnston's water tower.

By September 17, the only remnant of the reservoir was the center support column. The "temporary" structure did not go down without a fight. The original concrete walls, webbed with steel mesh and bars, provided a challenge to the wrecking crew. The steel beam replacement roof, designed by Iowa State College (now Iowa State University) engineers in the late 1930s, failed to crumble with the walls and remained like a giant wagon wheel resting on the center support.

The Camp Dodge swimming pool, listed on the National Register of Historic Places in 1995, continued to be a popular summer spot through the 1990s. Not only was the pool used by the public, it was also used in military training. Seen below, a group of soldiers conduct survival training. Unfortunately much-needed repairs to the aging structures, the high cost of liability insurance, increased post security requirements, and the changing tastes of the public all conspired to close the historic pool complex in 2002.

Although the swimming pool itself could no longer be used, it was decided to preserve the pool complex layout. The bathing pavilion's interior was redesigned for use as classrooms and a meeting hall. The WPA-era concession stand, which had been enclosed, is scheduled to be remodeled to reflect its original concept design. The pool's perimeter outline will be retained and its open view and grassed hillside will be maintained. In the fall of 2008, the rumble of trucks replaced the shouts of swimmers as gravel, fabric liner, and soil were set in place. After a 75-year run, the pool was no more.

Some Camp Dodge landmarks just needed a change of scenery and a bit of a makeover for the new millennium. In 2006, the Iowa Air National Guard A-7D Corsair, on display at the Beaver Drive tank park, was in need of a new paint job. It was disengaged from its display pedestal and flown out by an Iowa Army National Guard CH-47 Chinook helicopter for painting at the Des Moines Airbase. The return process, three weeks later, was as challenging as its trip out. The jet was airlifted back and placed at the base of tank park hill, moved onto a truck by Camp Dodge maintenance personnel and Iowa Guard soldiers, then moved up the hill. Finally it was successfully placed, by crane, onto its original concrete pedestal.

With the completion of the STARC Armory in 1994, the office of the adjutant general moved out of its 1950s-era building and moved into the new facility. The vacated headquarters building was occupied by the Iowa Gold Star Military Museum, formerly housed in the lower level of the Camp Dodge Memorial Building. Changes for the museum are underway, with the construction of a $4 million addition, seen on the right behind the plane, in this March 2009 photograph. Seen below, workers erect support beams and construct block walls that will connect the present museum structure to the new addition.

Inspired by the 1918 Statue of Liberty photograph taken at Camp Dodge, state employees assemble in the Miller Armory parking lot to form the shape of the state of Iowa. Many employees wore blue T-shirts displaying the red, white, and blue troop support ribbons. Copy prints were mailed to Iowa troops in Kuwait and Iraq to show support for their efforts in Operation Desert Storm.

Adj. Gen. Warren G. Lawson (left) congratulates a soldier at an IMA graduation ceremony around 1990. A Fairfield native, Lawson served as adjutant general from 1985 until his retirement in 1999.

Personnel from the Iowa Homeland Security and Emergency Management Division (HSEMD) assemble at the SEOC in the heart of the Joint Forces Headquarters building. HSEMD conducts regular exercises to assure statewide readiness for emergencies and disasters. In addition, the division ensured preparedness for the changeover to the year 2000. (Courtesy of Iowa HSEMD.)

Vice Pres. Dick Cheney visited Camp Dodge on July 17, 2006, to offer words of praise for the Iowa Army and Air National Guard's role in the War on Terror. Cheney spoke at the National Maintenance Training Center. Seated directly behind Vice President Cheney in the front row are Iowa governor Thomas Vilsack and Iowa adjutant general Ron Dardis.

As part of its land stewardship responsibilities, the Iowa National Guard strives to protect the post's cultural resources. Extensive archaeological surveys have been conducted at Camp Dodge in order to identify and preserve both historic and prehistoric resources. In the autumn of 2005, archaeologists conduct soil testing at the site of the World War I Civic Center (above). In the image below, the woods near Beaver Creek shelter the foundations of the World War I incinerator building.

In order to share and celebrate Camp Dodge history, various events are planned for the public and the press. During a 2005 "Media Day," held at a World War I archaeological dig site, Iowa Gold Star Military Museum director Russell Bierl discusses the post's history with a representative from the Weitz Company, which had played a major role in the construction of World War I Camp Dodge.

S.Sgt. Daryl Heldt, Iowa National Guard, drives a World War I 1918 Liberty standard truck while wearing the helmet of his World War I veteran grandfather. The truck, left behind as surplus by the U.S. Army following World War I, is one of only two still operating in the United States and is maintained by the Iowa Gold Star Military Museum.

Perhaps the most bittersweet moments in Camp Dodge's history are homecomings. These events are visible reminders of the reason that the Iowa National Guard and Camp Dodge exist, giving service to community, state, and nation. In the image above, members of the Headquarters and Headquarters Detachment, 34th Military Police Battalion, the last Iowa unit to return from Operation Desert Storm, greet waiting loved ones. Both men and women now don the military uniform and face combat. A lone cavalry horseman, seen below, rides again on Camp Dodge soil, honoring the 2008 return of Troop A, 1-113th Cavalry, after service in Iraq. Bagpipers lead the soldiers as eager friends and family members look on.

BIBLIOGRAPHY

Boot, Kyle J. "With Us Still . . . The Camp Dodge Story," Johnston, IA: Iowa Gold Star Military Museum, 2005.

"Camp Dodge: Where Iowa Meets the Army." Camp Dodge Induction Station photograph album. Camp Dodge: Iowa Gold Star Military Museum Library, 1943.

Douglas, Bill. "Wartime Illusions and Disillusionment: Camp Dodge and Racial Stereotyping, 1917–1918." *Annals of Iowa* (Spring 1998): 111–134.

Foradas, James G., Camilla Deiber, and K. Kris Hirst. "Archaeological Investigation of Components of the 13th Cantonment of World War I, Camp Dodge, Polk County, Iowa." Marion, Iowa: Louis Berger Group, October 2004.

Haynes, Fred E. "Social Work at Camp Dodge." *Iowa Journal of History and Politics* (October 1918): 471–547.

Jacobson, James E. "The Iowa National Guard from the Bottom Up: Community Participation in the Guard, 1839–1955." Johnston, IA: Iowa National Guard, 2006.

"Our Sons at Camp Dodge." *Des Moines Register and Tribune*, 1917.

Powers, Col. Orson B. Camp Dodge Induction Station photograph album. Camp Dodge: Iowa Gold Star Military Museum Library, 1944.

Pownall, Dorothy Ashby. "A Girl Reporter at Camp Dodge." *Palimpsest* (June 1966).

Shelby, I. P. "Completion Report of Camp Dodge, Des Moines, Iowa." Camp Dodge: Office of the Constructing Quartermaster, 1919.

United States of America. "Survey of Camp Dodge, Herrold, Iowa, To Determine the Present Condition of the Premises for Transfer From The State of Iowa to the United States of America Under Lease Dated May 23, 1942." 1942.